DON'T AVOID THE GAPS

How to create and lead through gaps in your organization

SCOTT PATCHIN

I0060421

Copyright © 2020 by Scott Patchin

This is a work of nonfiction.

All rights reserved by the author, including the
right of reproduction in whole or in part in any form.

Cover design and Layout by S.Y Lee-Wan
Editing and Publishing by Jen Hayes

ISBN: 978-1-7331346-4-4

Don't Avoid the Gaps

A workbook to help you create and lead through gaps in your organization.

Who this is for:

Executive leaders. Leaders in any part of an organization that are striving for growth and impact.

A growth-minded leader is someone aspiring to be more influential in driving the long-term impact of the work of their team, and who is preparing themselves to lead a team where others are managing the day-to-day while they have ownership over strategy and managing larger changes.

What it will do:

Provide a lens to see your leadership role in a bigger and different way. With that new view and understanding, apply it to the work of your team by challenging them, engaging them in the conversation, and working to support their growth and success.

Why I wrote this:

Too often I see leaders pursue a solution because someone they trust told them it would help – and it doesn't. The main reason this happens is because the leader did not sit back and think about WHY they need to do something different in their business.

The goal of this workbook is to equip leaders with a simple way to understand the role they are being asked to play and develop a path for mastering the three gaps. Leadership is not easy, and yet by focusing on specific actions, the path to mastery can start tomorrow.

The goal of this workbook is to equip leaders with a simple way to understand the role they are being asked to play and develop a path for mastering the three gaps.

Introduction

Leading through Gaps

*What is leadership?
Leadership is the
ability to create and
successfully manage
the closing of gaps.*
Scott Patchin

,,

One of my first leadership lessons occurred two decades ago when I was traveling in Europe (though the significance of the moment didn't dawn on me until years later).

I was in London, standing at a Tube station (what we would refer to stateside as a 'subway station'), waiting for a train. As the train arrived and the doors opened, I heard a disembodied female voice from above declare, "Mind the gap!" My initial reaction was a smile and a chuckle because of the British accent and the puzzling command. After thinking about it for a moment, I realized that she was advising me to watch my step in order to avoid injury while boarding the train from the platform. I listened, I saw the gap that needed to be managed, and I took the appropriate step to successfully navigate the gap.

Twenty-two years later, I was preparing a presentation to a group of individuals charged with helping leaders in Michigan to grow their businesses. I was looking at my definition of leadership and the tools I had developed to help leaders – not only to grow their businesses but also to develop their own capacities as leaders. As I reflected on my hundreds of conversations with leaders and all the books, TED talks, speakers, and classes which I had experienced, I recalled that moment in London and it hit me:

The basic challenge of leadership, whether leading others or leading yourself, comes down to creating and managing the gaps—the spaces between where we are and where we want to be.

What is a gap?

A gap is the space between where we are and where we want to go. Sometimes it's as simple as stepping onto a subway car, but in business it becomes a complex exercise to determine precisely what your current state is and to use some of those same measures to define a future state.

The second thing that hit me is that *Mind the gap!* was a warning.

Far too often, I've met leaders who saw the presence of a gap as something to avoid or a problem that had to be blamed on someone else. Carol Dweck helped put this issue into perspective for me in her book *Mindset: The New Psychology of Success* in which she shares her research that has identified fixed and growth mindsets. A fixed-mindset person is focused on looking good and proving their worth with effort. A growth-mindset person is someone who sees potential as something that continues to be stretched and grown through seeking challenges, learning through the difficult journey of delivering on a commitment, and perceives a negative outcome as the first step to doing it better next time.

Creating and managing gaps comes much more naturally to growth-mindset people. Fixed-mindset individuals are going to struggle to embrace this approach, as it goes against their grain. It's critical that we all have honest self-assessment. If leading through gaps makes you uncomfortable, I encourage you to read Carol Dweck's book, which offers valuable insight and advice that can help you grow to the point where you come to see gaps as opportunities to lead and learn.

The Three Gaps to Master

I work with leaders and organizations primarily at growth transition points.

This work has connected me with hundreds of leaders challenged with steering a growing organization or with promotion to a leadership role. Through all these experiences, I've become convinced that the simple lesson I learned in London years ago contains a key message for leaders: *effective leadership is about gap management.*

There are three key gaps every leader must master for effective leadership:

1. Creating a performance gap for your organization (aka, *strategic planning*).

2. Managing the gap in your organizational performance (aka, *operational planning*).

3. Managing the individual performance gap created by the previous two steps (aka, *leadership or individual development*).

Gap #1

Creating a Performance Gap for Your Organization
(Strategic Planning)

Greg McCann concisely illustrated the impact of working together to solve a business problem while team-building: "If the relationships matter, then process trumps outcome."

"

The concept of creating a gap may at first glance seem counterintuitive. You could fairly ask, "Why would I deliberately create a space that separates me from where I want to be?"

The foundation of this concept is that leaders deliberately create goals for the future that in turn create gaps for companies, teams, and individuals. A leader must, in essence, create a gap in the process of goal-setting and strategic planning.

The creation of a performance gap follows a two-step process:

Step #1: Define where you want to be in 3 to 5 years.
A simple way of looking at the future for your organization is to pick a date 3 to 5 years in the future. Imagine yourself at an all-company meeting someday, standing in front of your team talking about successes over the past 3 to 5 years. In this scenario:

- **What are you celebrating?**

- **As you look around at your facilities, products, customers, and people, what do you see?**

- **What is your role in the company?**

- **What are the business's metrics for sales, gross profit, net income, and number of people?**

This concept is directly applicable to the planning process. Answering these questions as you look ahead to that desired future will create a list of ten to fifteen bullet points that define the things you would like to see and specific results that you will use to measure the health of the business.

The gap gets created when, for each one of those statements, you answer the question: "What is the current state?" (If you're unsure, just answer with a great big "?")

This exercise creates the performance gap for your organization and is the foundation of strategic planning. It's that simple, and, like many of the things leaders do, it's not that easy. It requires you to:

- Bring a group of leaders into a room to get their opinion.

- Listen and be open to input from others.

- Share specific and sometimes sensitive information to help define a clearer picture of the performance of the business (e.g., profit and margin numbers).

- Be willing and capable of taking a critical look at the current strengths and weaknesses of all the leaders (including you) and the organization.

It also needs to get completed, which means resisting the temptation to make the language perfect and to create an endless loop of analysis that paralyzes the process. Trust your judgement and make a need for more detailed analysis a goal for the next quarter. Your outcome should be a vision for the future that creates clarity for the team.

Step #2: Create the same picture for 12 months from now.
The next step for creating the performance gap is to look at the current state versus the future state and ask everyone: "What has to change and/or get done in the next 12 months to launch our journey toward this vision?"

Have each team member come up with three to five goals for the organization and write them on a 4x6 sticky note. This size note is key to ensuring that everyone has an equal chance to share their ideas by limiting their thoughts to what will fit on the note. This will help to level the playing field for introverts versus extroverts, sales versus operations, entrepreneur versus leadership team, and any other dynamic that could threaten the balance between listening and talking.

The most effective teams allow different members to lead as the tasks around planning evolve, while everyone stays engaged to participate with and support the work at each step.

Does one person doing the work while everyone else is looking at their phones say *teamwork?* No, it says *your work.*

Use the process to set the expectations of teamwork for the team, and as a way of leveraging and recognizing the strengths of individual team members. Strong teams are those that cultivate and leverage diversity of thought. The process of strategic planning can be a team-building activity if each leader stays engaged and is willing to lead or follow at various points in the process.

Make Your Action Plan

Step #1: Define where you want to be in 3 to 5 years.

Pick a date 3 to 5 years in the future. Imagine yourself at an all-company meeting, standing in front of your team talking about successes over the past 3 to 5 years.

What are you celebrating?

As you look around at your facilities, products, customers, and people, what do you see?

What are the business's metrics for sales, gross profit, net income, and number of people?

What is your role in the company?

Step #2: Create the same picture for 12 months from now.

What has to change and/or get done in the next 12 months to launch our journey toward this vision?

Step #3: Get the team involved.

Have each team member come up with three to five goals for the organization and write them on a 4x6 sticky note. This size note is key to ensuring that everyone has an equal chance to share their ideas by limiting their thoughts to what will fit on the note.

Gap #2

Managing the Gap in Your Organizational Performance
(Operational Planning)

Me:	In my standard way of getting to know a new client and his or her leadership practices, I started our first meeting by asking, "What's your experience around strategic planning?"
Leader:	He quickly pointed to a folder on the shelf above his desk and shared a story about partnering with a major university and working diligently through their process to come up with this plan.
Me:	My next question was, "How have you used it, and what's been the impact?"
Leader:	He shrugged and said, "I haven't opened it in a year, so I guess the simple answer is that it hasn't made an impact."

Having a long-term plan with no strategy in place to execute it is worthless.

The key to successfully managing the organizational-performance gap is to develop a plan with a clear long-term goal (12 months) alongside well-defined steps outlined for the short-term work (30 to 90 days), which are needed to move toward achievement of the ultimate goal.

If the big rocks don't go in first, they aren't going to fit in later.

Stephen Covey

"

The path to successfully managing this gap follows a four-step process:

Step #1: Write down an essential rock for your next 90 days.
While goals are longer term (6-12 months), I like to use the term introduced by Stephen Covey and used by the likes of business thought leaders Gino Wickman and Verne Harnish – rocks. Rocks are specific things that need to get done in the next 90 days. Limit the description of the rock to no more than twenty to forty words. It is critical to have a rock that has a clear measure of success, a single owner, and a due date. This is one of those simple-but-not-easy tasks. Clarity can only be defined by looking at the rock 30 days later and having a concrete, clear definition of what successful completion of the rock would look like.

As the leader, is pulling the detail of a plan together and keeping track of changes one of your strengths? I worked with an organization where the most organized person was not the leader, so this person took on the duty of running the weekly meetings and tracking the issues and commitments that came out of each meeting.

The benefit? The leader was humble enough to admit their weaknesses and a key team member stepped up, sharing their strengths for the betterment of the team. This is an example of using the planning and leading process as a way to strengthen relationships.

Step #2: Ensure that the owner of the rock understands it, wants to do it, and has the strengths, experience, support, and time to complete it.

We've all committed to rocks that we had no idea how to accomplish. Remember the energy around saying "yes" and the paralyzing fear minutes or hours later when you realize that you have no idea how to do it? It's true that leaders have to figure things out, but full or partial failure on major tasks can sink an organization. It is essential that a leader has the confidence to say, "I don't know" or "I need help."

Step #3: Create a rhythm of checking on progress and problem-solving any issues that arise.

Create a routine of regular progress check-ins, and solving problems created by challenging rocks/goals and a changing business environment as they arise. This is where the real ability of leaders to argue, listen, think, and act will be created and tested. The most effective leadership teams meet weekly to solve the big issues and to continually monitor progress toward the most important goals. Embrace the mantra: "95% done is not done."

Step #4: Be a micro-supporting manager, not a micro-manager.

Create time to dive into the details of the rock with others. While leaders must trust their peers' ability to plan and execute a rock, it's important that someone reviews the details to provide input, challenge assumptions, and bring a different perspective to the solution. This is not micro-managing, it's micro-supporting. All leaders should expect this from their peers and certainly from their teams. Large or complex rocks should be reviewed by the entire leadership team.

Writings on leadership will often delineate distinctions between leadership and management. The most essential thing to understand about the difference between these two concepts is that *leaders* create gaps for organizations, teams, and individuals and then provide sufficient resources to successfully manage those gaps, while *managers* work with people and organizational resources to effectively manage day-to-day operations to ensure that goals are achieved on a daily and weekly basis.

Tip: Remember, leaders create gaps for organizations, teams, and individuals and then provide sufficient resources to successfully manage those gaps.

Make Your Action Plan

Step #1: Write down an essential rock for your next 90 days.

Step #2: Does the owner of the rock...

- ...understand it?

- ...want to do it?

- ...have the strength, experience, support, and time to complete it?

Step #3: Create a routine of regular progress check-ins to solve problems created by challenging rocks / goals and a changing business environment as they arise.

Check-in rhythm (circle one; weekly is recommended): Weekly / Biweekly

Date to begin:

Amount of time:

Step #4: Be a micro-supporting manager, not a micro-manager.

Have all rocks been reviewed by others?
Remember to provide input, challenge assumptions, and bring a different perspective to the solution.

Gap #3:

Managing the Individual Performance Gap Created by the Previous Two Steps
(Leadership Development / Individual Development)

A plan that stretches the organization creates fertile ground for the growth of people. Growth-minded leaders see challenges as opportunities.

Scott Patchin

This is the single biggest issue in any business, but especially in the high-growth organizations that I work with. Framing this concept in terms of leadership development (for the sake of simplicity), there are two truths to observe:

1. The formula for effective leadership can be summarized thus: my capacity as a leader + my capacity as a manager + the capacity of my team ≥ the accountabilities of my role + the accountabilities of the strategic plan I own + anything else that happens to impact our plan.

2. Effective leadership development in a growing organization is based on the premise that my capacity as a leader is increasing faster than the leadership needs of my team and the organization.

A couple of points merit special attention.

First, the definition of effective leadership must include your team. The single biggest reason that most entrepreneurial companies fail to grow beyond ten people is that the leader is the chief doer who either is content with the status quo or cannot leverage the true talents of their team to grow the business.

In John Maxwell's book, *The 21 Irrefutable Laws of Leadership: Follow Them and People Will Follow You,* Law #1 is the 'Law of the Lid'. Maxwell states that, "If your leadership rates an 8, then your effectiveness can never be greater than a 7. Your leadership ability – for better or worse – always determines your effectiveness and the potential impact of your organization."

Second, training is typically not mentioned anywhere in leadership development. Leaders in growing organizations need to own their own development and find ways to learn on the job. Training is a part of the solution, but studies have shown that only ten percent of learning happens in the classroom, so we must create learning opportunities in our work.

The two key conditions required for the creation of these learning opportunities:

1. Trusting relationships that allow truth to be spoken through feedback

2. The leader's ability to ask for help

Whether the goal is succession planning, developing future leaders, or addressing the leadership needs of a growing organization, using these formulas to assess the performance of leaders in their roles will tell you whether or not a gap exists or will exist in the future.

The path to successfully managing the individual performance gap consists of committing to and developing four habits. My experience of working with hundreds of leaders and individuals has convinced me that if these habits are in place, chances are that individual performance gaps are being effectively managed.

Habit #1:
Create a rigorous selection process to ensure that no leader is given a role that they don't have the capacity to perform. Alternatively, have a plan in place to support the leader while they build that capacity. This applies to both internal promotions and external hires.

Habit #2:
Create a high-trust environment at the leadership-team level in which members provide feedback to each other at least quarterly to recognize progress toward development goals. Reset development goals annually. High trust also exists if leadership team members are meeting one-on-one to check in with and support each other (i.e., fostering friendships). In my experience, if a team doesn't practice either of these behaviors, the trust level is too low for the team to be able to have the kind of healthy conflict that is required to make effective decisions..

Habit #3:
Conduct one-on-ones between the CEO and leadership team members annually to create development plans, quarterly to review progress, and monthly or bi-weekly for micro-supporting conversations.

Habit #4:
Connect each member of the leadership team to a peer group that meets a couple of times per year and/or ensure that each member has met with a mentor in the past 18 months. In my experience with leadership teams, one of the primary barriers to teamwork in the C-suite is ego. Performing this habit provides a form of support for a leader that is often viewed as safer because it is with an outside group of peers or a more experienced leader. It also creates a strong network around your leaders to support their own ability to see megatrends in the market and become more aware of partnership opportunities.

Your notes:

This is the forgotten gap. I once had a leader question the need for my services because he "hired leaders who can figure it out." My response was simple. "They can figure it out, but at what cost to your bottom line and human capital?" I could tell by his expression that I hit a nerve with that question. It's an expensive lesson, for example, to turn over one or two highly skilled individuals or to make mistakes that impact the profit of the organization by even ten percent.

The existence of trust does not necessarily mean they like one another, it means they understand one another

Peter Drucker

99

Make Your Action Plan

Apply this formula to your leadership:

My capacity as a leader + my capacity as a manager + the capacity of my team ≥
the accountabilities of my role + the accountabilities of the strategic plan I own + anything
else that happens to impact our plan

Questions to ask yourself

1. When you are open and honest with yourself, are the elements on the left side greater than the elements on the right side?

2. If NO, then what do you have to change to make this a true statement for you and your team?

Commit to and develop these four habits:

Habit #1:
Develop a rigorous selection process for each leader.

Habit #2:
Create a high-trust environment at the leadership-team level in which members provide feedback to each other at least quarterly to recognize progress towards development goals.

Habit #3:
Conduct one-on-ones between the CEO and leadership team members annually to create development plans, quarterly to review progress, and monthly or bi-weekly for micro-supporting conversations.

Habit #4:
Connect each member of the leadership team to a peer group that meets a couple of times per year and/or ensure that each member has met with a mentor in the past eighteen months.

Gap X:
Owning the Gap

*Whether you think
you can, or you
think you can't –
you're right."*

Henry Ford

,,

I've written about the challenges that the leaders I work with face in owning their gaps in my workbook *Own It*. The importance of 'owning it' bears mention at this point. Think about what you're doing (or not doing) to own the individual performance gaps that appear when your leaders and teams create gaps by creating plans and working to manage those gaps.

To assist in this self-reflection, answer the questions:

- **What gaps do I see in my own performance?**

- **What gaps do I see in my teams' performance?**

- **What can I do to assist in closing these gaps?**

- **What help do I need from my teams in closing these gaps?**

Taking ownership of your gaps can be achieved in two steps:

1. Recognize that any performance gaps that exist are yours to own. The simple act of asking the four questions above creates ownership by demonstrating three critical behaviors: willingness to ask for help, willingness to accept feedback, and willingness and ability to follow through on commitments.

2. Proactively build your capacity to lead before that capacity is needed. Acknowledge the value of career development and of knowing what future opportunities are available. Create a written plan or go through my 2-month process to create a career plan.

Make Your Action Plan

Reflect on your own development:

What gaps do I see in my own performance?

What gaps do I see in my teams' performance?

What can I do to assist in closing these gaps?

What help do I need from my teams in closing these gaps?

Proactively build your capacity to lead before that capacity is needed. Acknowledge the value of career development and of knowing what future opportunities are available. Create a written plan or go through my 2-month process to create a career plan.

Next Steps: Make Your Action Plan

Your first step on the path to creating and managing your gaps can be taken by answering the questions:

What do you believe leadership is?

What part of this gap discussion resonates most strongly with you?

Around which piece do you most want to increase your capacity and/or your team's capacity to lead?

What area does your leader need to focus on most?

A second step would be to take the self-assessment at the end of this document to identify some specific gaps that exist for your organization and for you as a leader.

Finally, I firmly believe that in great organizations everybody leads. I leave you with a quote to illustrate that **leader** is more than just a title:

Leaders have followers.
Managers have employees.
Managers make widgets.
Leaders make change.

Seth Godin

,,

My hope is that, from wherever you sit in your organization, you will see those gaps, create those gaps, and make change.

More about TrUst and TrUth from Scott

When I launched my consulting business in 2009, I became that consultant across the table from leaders. I was faced with posing the big questions: "What problem are you trying to solve?" and "What's keeping you up at night?" I found that leaders tend to identify problems clustered around their perceived needs, rather than asking how to improve their own leadership capabilities.

From my two decades of working with leaders and studying leadership, two truths have emerged:

1. If your leadership journey is driven by the latest book, you will end up spending too much time chasing someone else's vision of leadership.

2. The most effective form of leadership development follows the formula: LEARNING + DOING = GROWTH.

With this epiphany, I defined one of my foundational philosophies of leadership and put it into my company's name. This two-pronged precept is central to the underlying philosophy, and name, of The trU Group; specifically, that the two things leaders must work at every day are building trUst – between the leader and the team, as well as within the team – and leveraging that trUst to get the trUth, in all its forms, on the table. (The 'U' is capitalized because, as a leader, for trust to exist and truth to emerge, you must first focus on 'U'. I firmly believe that being a people-centered leader is essential to effective servant leadership.)

The two things leaders must work at every day are building trUst and leveraging that trUst to get the trUth on the table - first focusing on 'U'.

Q & A

Questions Leaders Often Ask

Q: What are the main threats to effectively managing the gaps in my organization?

A: In my experience of working with leadership teams, I have found three main things that will sink your ability to effectively manage gaps. It's important that every leader understands these potential pitfalls from the beginning of the process and actively works to minimize or eliminate these threats every day.

1. **Lack of Trust:** In an executive team, lack of trust manifests as leaders not asking for help before it's too late – usually because they feel like they should be able to do it on their own and they have a big title. Another manifestation occurs in leaders who are unwilling to ask questions of their peers if they don't understand the progress that's being made, or who question whether the progress is on-schedule based solely on what they see or hear without delving deeper.

2. **Lack of Competency or Commitment:** When we assign work to people who lack the skills, time, or energy to complete it, the work does not get done. I watch for leaders who ask for help and teams that openly and professionally question the ability of a peer to finish a critical task. This is a critical moment with trust and truth that will make all the difference.

3. **Lack of Meeting Time:** If a leadership team doesn't hold meetings at least weekly, with quarterly and annual reviews, the managing part of gap management never gets done well. Another potential pitfall is that the team only meets when the leader is there to run it. Both situations are threats to managing the gap effectively.

Questions to ask:

Q: Leadership matters. But what is it?

A: Every leader I talk to, at any level of an organization, agrees on one thing: leadership is critical for the success of an organization. It makes or breaks us, individually and collectively, and we've all had firsthand experience with leaders who either brought out the best or worst in everyone around them.

But why? While we can all agree on how important effective leadership is, I find little agreement or clarity on how to achieve it. Far too often, the path to good leadership is defined by the consultant sitting in front of you. Leadership training has become a multi-billion-dollar business, resulting in leaders following the latest book or fad. In fact, a simple Amazon search for books on leadership today yields more than 175,000 choices! No wonder leaders feel overwhelmed by conflicting advice.

I always encourage leaders to define for themselves what they think leadership is, then ask them to use the training they receive to refine their own definition. This workbook is about helping you, as a leader, develop your understanding of what effective leadership looks like and how it translates into developing the people around you, who are critical to your success.

Make Your Action Plan

Self-Assessment

How are you doing? This assessment will help you see the gaps and create plans to close them.

Gap #1: Creating a Performance Gap for Your Organization (Strategic Planning).

1. We have a written long-term plan (3-5 years) for the organization.
    YES/NO

2. We have written short-term goals for the organization to accomplish in the next year.
    YES/NO

3. We have set sales and income goals for the organization for 1 year and for 3-5 years that the leadership team has reviewed and approved.
    YES/NO

If you answered, "No" to any of these questions, you are not doing the work as leaders to create the performance gap for your organization. If you want to explore this gap in greater depth, I encourage you to use my *Demystifying Strategic Planning* workbook or review one of the following for some ideas:

*   *Building Your Company's Vision* by James C. Collins and Jerry I. Porras (Harvard Business Review)
*   *Can You Say What Your Strategy Is?* by David J. Collis and Michael G. Rukstad (Harvard Business Review)
*   *Traction: Get a Grip on Your Business* by Gino Wickman

Gap #2: Managing the Gap in Your Organizational Performance (Operational Planning).

1. We have the work defined by quarter to achieve the annual goals.
    YES/NO

2. Each of the goals in this quarter has a single owner, a due date, and a clear definition of what "done" means for the goal.
    YES/NO

3. The leadership team meets weekly to review the progress of quarterly goals and our weekly scorecard.
    YES/NO

4. The leadership team meets quarterly to set or reset the goals for the next quarter.
    YES/NO

5. We have a history of achieving 75% or more of our annual goals.
   YES/NO

6. We have a budget in place and metrics that we review at least monthly.
   YES/NO

If you answered "No" to any of these questions, you are not doing the work as leaders to manage the organizational performance gap by defining the work that must occur and effectively managing changes and problems that arise. If you want to explore this gap in greater depth, please contact me for a complimentary copy of my whitepaper on strategic planning. I have also included a list of resources at the end of this document that I often share with clients on this journey.

Gap #3: Managing the Individual Performance Gap Created by the Previous Two Steps (Leadership Development/Individual Development).

1. I delivered annual evaluations to all of my direct reports on time.
   YES/NO

2. I have one-on-one discussions with each of my direct reports at least once a month.
   YES/NO

3. Each of my direct reports has a development plan.
   YES/NO

4. I would gladly rehire all of my direct reports into their current roles.
   YES/NO

If you answered "No" to any of the first three questions, you are not doing the work as leader to develop the capacity of your team to become more effective at their roles. A key item to remember is that the habits you create with your leaders are more likely to be repeated by them with their teams. If you have bad habits, those will become the norm for the rest of your organization. I offer 30-minute conversations with any leaders struggling with this to help think through a plan to move from no to yes on these questions. Contact me via email (scott@thetrugroup.com) or phone (616.405.1018).

If you answered "No" to question #4, your job is doubtless harder because you have to spend too much of your time and energy supporting the performance of underperforming team members. The question that must be addressed in this instance is whether it is a case of the right person in the wrong seat or the wrong person in the right seat.

Your Planning Framework
The Honest Culture Journey

> *Plans help leaders move the organization, but being involved in the planning is the key step in getting the 21st century team member to own it and drive it. If you want extra passion and effort, include them!*
>
> Scott Patchin
>
> 99

Strategic planning is a journey. Using the lens of honest culture to manage it will make the outcomes so much more powerful and the journey so much more energizing.

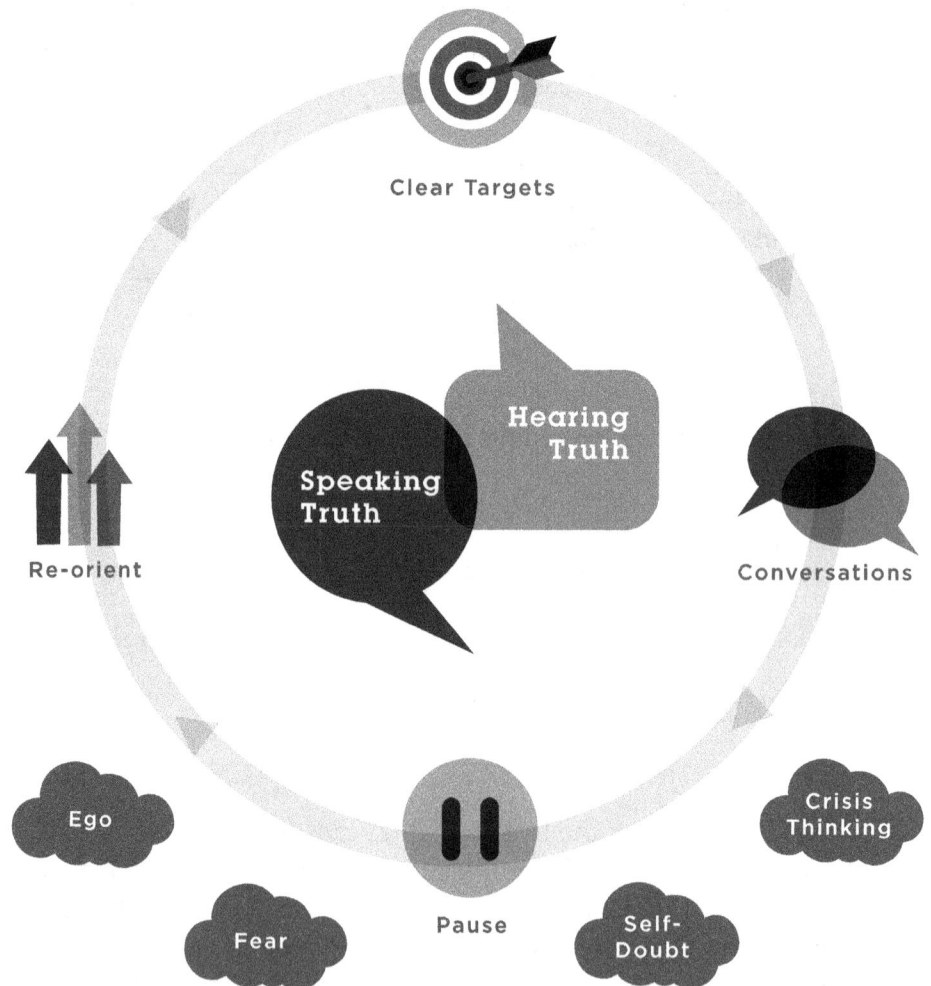

The center of the Honest Culture Journey is speaking truth and hearing truth. This is at the heart of the work. To the extent it happens, the journey becomes a place where respect is given and felt, which is a key ingredient to a healthy and high-performing team. Trust and respect are accelerators to success.

To get you started, here is how the key events go together:

Clear Targets

Every journey has a destination – whether it is physical, spiritual, or emotional. There is always a reason. When a team is involved, it provides the foundation for the relationships from the very beginning. It starts with the simple question: "Why are we doing this?" Then it gets to the other key pieces of information – the who? what? where? when? and how? of our journey. There are two more key questions to answer, but this gets us started.

Conversations

Our journey joins the need to achieve something and the relationship outcome of doing it as a team. This step is about all the interactions that just happen when we journey together. Things like same room/same time connections, instant texts or emails, or even slow connections such as dangling texts, unresolved emails, or other barriers to our sense of immediacy.

Pause

Journeys are fraught with movement, emotions, shortages, and lots of rerouting. The pause is an intentional event to slow down and focus people on speaking truth and, even more importantly, hearing truth. It can be a one-to-one, leader-to-many, or a team pause (three to eight people). There is no time limit, only the objective to quiet the noise of the journey to speak and hear truth from each other. An effective pause creates an emotionally safe place for all to share and a physical space to allow all to focus.

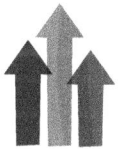

Re-orient

Effective journeys go beyond the simple question of "Are we there yet?" to the powerful questions of "How far have we gone?" and "What will it take to finish the journey?" This step is the action step after the pause to reset the picture of what? where? when? and how? with the most critical step to assign or reassign the who? involved. As roles and tasks shift on a journey, it is important for all teams and individuals to have clarity and alignment on the work ahead. Reorient makes sure that happens.

There are four things that will obstruct your journey and cause it to fail, either through an inability to see, missed steps, or ignoring others on your journey. I call these clouds, and they come in four forms:

Ego: Too much or too little is the issue here. The key signs are statements like, "They can't..." or "They won't..."

Fear: It either has a paralyzing effect or causes you to make big, quick, and often reckless decisions without considering any input from others.

Self-doubt: It can sound a lot like too little Ego, but the biggest challenge is getting people to speak up and share. This cloud causes people to disappear.

Crisis thinking: It is often rooted in fear, and moves decision-making to the amygdala or, as Seth Godin calls it, 'The Lizard Brain'. This is most commonly called the 'fight-or-flight' response.

Visit thetrugroup.com/honest-culture-journey to learn more about the tools I have created to equip you for this journey and to get on a list to hear more.

www.ingramcontent.com/pod-product-compliance
Lightning Source LLC
Chambersburg PA
CBHW051405200326
41520CB00024B/7504